WEATHERMAN

A COMEDY

D1197557

by

JERRY POLNER

SAMUEL FRENCH, INC.

45 WEST 25TH STREET   NEW YORK 10010

7623 SUNSET BOULEVARD HOLLYWOOD 90046

LONDON   TORONTO

CHARACTERS

ELIOT
MITZI
ROXANNE
BAGGAGE
LEONARD
NORMA

SYNOPSIS OF SCENES

The entire action of the play takes place in the office of the executive director of the National Weather Service, Washington, D.C. The time is the present.

ACT I

Scene 1
A seasonably warm Friday in August.

Scene 2
The following Monday morning.

ACT II

Scene 1
Three days later, afternoon.

Scene 2
One hour later, inside MITZI's supply closet.

Scene 3
That evening.

WEATHERMAN

ACT I

Scene 1

ELIOT and MITZI are alone onstage.

ELIOT. Are you telling me that you're not happy with your job?

MITZI. I didn't say that. It's just the filing part. I just don't like the filing.

ELIOT. Mitzi, I'm an executive director. And I've decided that I have to have files. An executive director has to have files. If I didn't have files, I'd be laughed out of the business.

MITZI. I know that, Eliot. And I feel really bad about it. But I just don't know what to do. I'm just not that good at it.

ELIOT. You have to develop some enthusiasm for your job, Mitzi. This isn't just a place to have office parties. This is the National Weather Service. We're talking about weather here.

MITZI. I know that, Eliot.

ELIOT. This isn't stocks and bonds, or oil wells, or computers. This is humidity, and slush, and freezing rain. This is really exciting stuff here.

MITZI. I'm excited about it. Really I am.

ELIOT. We have a very important mission in this agency. Because the weather is important. Every wind, every cloud, every storm. They're all important.

MITZI. I know that, Eliot. But what are we supposed to do about it? I mean it's just there, right? It isn't going to change.

ELIOT. Do we know that? Are we sure of that?

MITZI. Well, no, but....

ELIOT. And that's why we have to keep watching, Mitzi. We have to keep watching the stars, and the tides, and the clouds.

MITZI. But what does that have to do with my job?

ELIOT. Well we can't all be watching. Some of us have to answer the phone. Some of us have to empty wastebaskets. And some of us have to do the filing. You knew that was part of the job when you came here.

MITZI. But you told me you wanted a secretary who was dynamic. That was the word you kept using. Dynamic.

ELIOT. Exactly. Because that's the watch-word of my administration. Dynamic. I want everything we do here to be dynamic.

MITZI. But there's nothing dynamic about filing, Eliot. It's the same every day.

ELIOT. Well that's what I told you. You have to figure out a way to make it dynamic.

MITZI. But I don't know how to do that. How about if I

take some time off to think about it?

ELIOT. Mitzi, I thought that you understood things here. I am personally hurt by this entire situation.

MITZI. Well I'm sorry, Eliot.

ELIOT. You lost my file on the Trade Winds, didn't you.

MITZI. I didn't say that.

ELIOT. But that's what this is leading up to, isn't it. That's why you don't want to do filing anymore.

MITZI. Look, I'm sure it'll turn up somewhere. I'll call the Wind Section.

ELIOT. The Wind Section doesn't have it. I called them.

MITZI. Well I'm sorry, okay?

ELIOT. You're sorry, you're sorry. That doesn't help anything.

MITZI. Well if you'd only leave everything in the file cabinet where it belongs, then we wouldn't have a problem.

ELIOT. What good does it do me if I have to leave it in the file cabinet? How am I supposed to read it?

MITZI. Well at least it wouldn't get lost.

ELIOT. Mitzi, a good executive director always knows when it's time to crack the whip.

MITZI. Yes, Eliot.

ELIOT. And if I have to crack the whip, God damn it, I'll crack the whip.

MITZI. Yes, Eliot.

ELIOT. And I'm starting to think that this is a whip-cracking situation here.

MITZI. If you say so, Eliot.

ELIOT. Do you think this office is a joke?

MITZI. No, Eliot.

ELIOT. Well that's what it's beginning to look like. It's beginning to look like you think this office is a joke. Well let me assure you of something, Mitzi. This office is not a joke.

MITZI. I've been here for three months. I haven't laughed once.

ELIOT. Well see that you don't.

MITZI. Yes, Eliot.

ELIOT. As for your request to be taken off filing, I just don't know. I'll have to think about it.

MITZI. Isn't there someone else who could take it over?

ELIOT. It's a very important task. We can't have just anybody do it.

MITZI. Well there must be somebody.

ELIOT. I don't know what to do. I can't handle this kind of pressure.

MITZI. Aw gee, Eliot....

ELIOT. I have to have help. I can't handle this alone.

MITZI. Oh Eliot...

ELIOT. Send Roxanne in. Maybe she can figure it out.

MITZI. Oh, Roxanne won't help. She wouldn't do anything that would help me.

ELIOT. Now I don't want to hear anything derogatory about Roxanne. She's a dedicated public servant. This office would not be what it is today if it weren't for Roxanne.

MITZI. She won't let us have office parties or anything.

ELIOT. There'll be no bickering between you and Roxanne. There's a possibility that I'll be going away for three days starting this afternoon, and if I do, Roxanne will be in charge.

MITZI. Oh no! Oh Eliot, you can't do that.

ELIOT. I want the two of you to get along, you understand?

MITZI. She won't let us do anything. We can't even have Monday afternoons off when she's in charge. It's ridiculous. When are we supposed to go to the beach?

ELIOT. Well, Roxanne has a different management style. But you can have your party. I promise you can have your party. Stop worrying about it. Send in Roxanne and I'll ask her about your filing problem.

MITZI. Aww, she isn't going to do anything to help me.

ELIOT. Mitzi, that was a direct order. Now send in Roxanne.

MITZI. Yes, Eliot. *(She leaves.)*

ELIOT. Oh how will I ever do it? How will I ever rise to the test? How will I ever climb that highest of mountains? Wade that deepest of oceans? Walk that hottest of deserts? How will I bring weather home to the people of this great country?

(enter ROXANNE)

ROXANNE. You must. And you will.

ELIOT. No, no, it's all too much! It's too grand! It's too much of a dream. To be director of the Service and to have you too. It's too much! It's just too much! I'm so enraptured. My heart is like a warm front over the Carribean. I .... I can't breathe! Oh Roxanne!

ROXANNE. Come to your desk, my darling. It'll be alright. *(She reclines on the desk at center.)*

ELIOT. It's too much. It's just too much. Look at this office. Look at this desk. Look at you.

ROXANNE. Look at me.

ELIOT. Oh Roxanne. You're a pocket of upper air moisture dancing above my head.

ROXANNE. And you're a lightning rod, without the rod.

ELIOT. You're a tornado over Texas. You're absolutely ravishing.

ROXANNE. Yes. I know.

ELIOT. You're perfect.

ROXANNE. Yes, Eliot. And you should leave everything in my hands. Nothing will go wrong. Go back to Illinois and speak at the commencement. Everyone is expecting you.

ELIOT. But that'll mean three whole days away. I can't take three days off.

ROXANNE. Yes you can my darling.

ELIOT. But does the weather take three days off? Of course not. The arctic winds keep blowing. The upper air keeps circulating. The high pressure areas keep building.

ROXANNE. But I'll be here to watch all that for you. That's what I'm here for. That's what an executive assistant does. And haven't I done a terrific job?

ELIOT. Oh yes, Roxanne, yes. I just look at you and I think of weather.

ROXANNE. Well of course. I can do anything.

ELIOT. I knew you'd be perfect for the job since the moment I first saw you that Spring morning, in my backyard. Lying underneath my rain gauge. I thought you were from heaven.

ROXANNE. I was.

ELIOT. I can't imagine having all of this. The National Weather Service .... and you.

ROXANNE. And me.

ELIOT. And you.

ROXANNE and ELIOT. A woman.

ELIOT. Roxanne, I .... I want you to forget all about last night.

ROXANNE. Which part did you want me to forget?

ELIOT. You know. That moment on the floor. When you took off your shoes for me.

ROXANNE. You mean when you started crying?

ELIOT. Yes. That's the moment.

ROXANNE. Why did you cry when I took off my shoes?

ELIOT. Because you were so beautiful.

ROXANNE. Yes, yes, of course I was. But that was no reason for you to start crying.

ELIOT. I was so happy. But Roxanne, you .... you must never tell anyone what I told you last night.

ROXANNE. It's our secret, darling.

ELIOT. Oh God you're so loyal and faithful, Roxanne.

ROXANNE. Yes. I know.

ELIOT. Maybe ... maybe it would be okay for me to go back to Illinois for a few days. It seems like you have a firm grip on things.

ROXANNE. Firm. Very firm.

ELIOT. I'm so happy with you.

ROXANNE. Yes, darling. And you'll be even happier still. The more you listen to me and the more you take my advice, the happier you'll be.

ELIOT. You really think I should spend the weekend in Illinois?

ROXANNE. It's what you deserve, darling. That's why I set it up for you.

ELIOT. But what about the Service?

ROXANNE. I can handle it. I have everything under control.

ELIOT. Oh but my petite snowflake, you're working too hard. I don't want you to work.

ROXANNE. For me, work is like play. Unpleasant work is like rain in Morocco. It doesn't exist.

ELIOT. Oh, but all the things I have to do for the trip.

ROXANNE. *(She gets up and goes to the closet.)* All you have to do is enjoy the flight.

ELIOT. I have to pack.

ROXANNE. *(She removes his suitcase from the closet.)* All packed.

ELIOT. I have to get a ticket.

ROXANNE. *(She takes an envelope from her suit pocket and hands it to him.)* It's all here.

ELIOT. I have to get to the airport.

ROXANNE. Your driver is waiting downstairs.

ELIOT. I have to walk to the elevator. *(ROXANNE lifts him up and begins to carry him to the door.)* I'll walk, I'll walk, it's okay. *(ROXANNE puts him down. He stands in the doorway.)* Oh Roxanne, my darling. Three days without you. How will I ever survive?

ROXANNE. Of course it will be unpleasant, pumpkin, but think of .... think of warm sleet.

ELIOT. Warm sleet?

ROXANNE. Yes, warm sleet.

ELIOT. That's sickening. That's horrid.

ROXANNE. Yes. That's what life will be like without me. Goodbye my darling. *(ELIOT leaves. ROXANNE closes the door.)*

(MITZI enters from the other direction.)

MITZI. Uhh Roxanne, could you take my calls for the rest of the day?

ROXANNE. Excuse me?

MITZI. I have to go mix the dip.

ROXANNE. No. No partying.

MITZI. Eliot promised us. And he's the boss.

ROXANNE. And you think that means that it's play-time? That you can stop all your work and begin spreading things on crackers?

MITZI. Yuh, why not.

ROXANNE. Well you can't.

MITZI. I bought a new pair of pants just for this party.

ROXANNE. That's a dress.

MITZI. So I'm not a careful shopper. So what.

ROXANNE. We have too much work to do. No party.

MITZI. Aw gee, Roxanne.

ROXANNE. No party. Now go back to work.

MITZI. This whole office is tired of working. We worked all day last Wednesday.

ROXANNE. While Eliot is gone, I'm in charge. And I say get back to work.

MITZI. You think you can just walk in here and take over?

ROXANNE. Yes. I do.

MITZI. What are you so gung-ho on work for? What are you up to? Baggage told me you had something up your sleeve.

ROXANNE. The only thing up my sleeve is the back of my hand, and you're going to feel it if you don't change your attitude. Do you want to go back on probation?

MITZI. No, Roxanne.

ROXANNE. I didn't think so. Well I'm nipping this in the bud. Get Baggage in here. I'm going to give the two of you a talking to.

MITZI. I didn't really mean what I said before about Baggage. I don't even remember what he told me.

ROXANNE. Oh can it, girlie. I'll jog your memory so bad you'll never forget it.

MITZI. *(picking up the phone)* I really didn't mean anything by it. *(into the phone)* Hello Rick? Roxanne would like to see you.

ROXANNE. I'll teach you to spread rumors.

MITZI. *(to ROXANNE)* He says he'll try to fit you in toward the end of the week.

ROXANNE. *(shouts)* YOU TELL HIM I WANT HIM IN HERE NOW!

(BAGGAGE enters.)

BAGGAGE. Rick Baggage here.

ROXANNE. Yes, I know your name.

BAGGAGE. That's my name. Rick Baggage.

ROXANNE. Sit down, Baggage.

BAGGAGE. Thank you. *(He sits down.)*

ROXANNE. You've been talking to Mitzi, haven't you.

BAGGAGE. *(to MITZI)* What did you tell her?

MITZI. We just talked about the party, that's all.

ROXANNE. You discussed something other than the party, didn't you.

BAGGAGE. Besides the party? Absolutely nothing.

ROXANNE. You're trying to hide something from me, Baggage, and I don't like it. You're spreading rumors about me that I don't appreciate. Confess now, and I'll go easy on you. But if I don't get the truth out of you today, you can forget about your career in weather forever.

BAGGAGE. You think I care? You think I care about your lousy high pressure areas? You think I'm in this for the weather? What a joke. I'm in this for me. Rick Baggage. Yuh, that's right. For me. Do you know how long I've sweated in this lousy stinking bureau? Seven weeks! Yuh, that's right. Seven weeks. And what have I gotten for it? A belt buckle with a thermometer in it. Well now it's my turn. Now it's Rick Baggage's turn. I should have been the executive assistant. Yuh, me. Rick Baggage. And I would have been the executive assistant if you hadn't come along. Eliot would have picked me if you weren't so ... so tall and tan and ... young and lovely. It would have been me yelling at the stupid secretaries. It would have been me dancing with the daughters of milk price support lobbyists at Georgetown parties. That's right. Me. Rick Baggage. There, I said it. Now you know. Now you know why

I hate you.

MITZI. Uhh, I think I have some filing to do.

ROXANNE. *(to MITZI)* Stay right where you are. I haven't intimidated you enough yet. *(to BAGGAGE)* Baggage, you're through. Pack up your .... your suitcases and clear out.

BAGGAGE. Not this time, Roxanne. Not so fast. You can't get rid of me that easy. Because I know who you are. I know where you came from. Everybody else thinks you're plain old Roxanne Sunshower. But I know better.

ROXANNE. You know nothing.

BAGGAGE. You're really from Florida, aren't you.

ROXANNE. Mitzi, go do your filing.

MITZI. Right.

BAGGAGE. Stay where you are, Mitzi.

MITZI. I could bring my filing in here, actually.

ROXANNE. Who told you I was from Florida?

BAGGAGE. You were known in every boxing gym in Tallahassee. The sweetheart of the flyweights.

MITZI. Oh wow.

ROXANNE. You're lying through your miserable teeth.

BAGGAGE. But then Tallahassee wasn't good enough for you. You wanted the big time. The big game, the big money. So you left the old town and headed for the bright lights of Sarasota. And that was where you met him. The biggest mobster in central Florida. Mickey Melinski.

MITZI. Oh wow.

ROXANNE. You're making all this up. You don't have a shred of proof.

BAGGAGE. *(Takes out a newspaper clipping and shows it to MITZI.)* I have the whole story. It's all in this article taken from the Sarasota Carp.

ROXANNE. Oh my God!

MITZI. *(reading the article)* Oh wow.

ROXANNE. Where did you get that?

MITZI. You were really a piece of scum, weren't you. *(ROXANNE cries.)*

BAGGAGE. Melinski found you in the gutter. He had always dreamed of finding a woman in the gutter and never had. Because the streets in Sarasota don't have any gutters. You had to dig your own gutter. When he found you, you were covered with mud. You had dug yourself to sleep. And Mickey took you in. He made you part of his operation. He introduced you to everything. Dope. Prostitution. Selling term papers. The whole banana. You became his eyes. His brains. His woman.

ROXANNE. That's not true! I was never his woman. There was a short period of time when I was his traveling companion.

BAGGAGE. According to this article in the Carp, you were his traveling companion even when he wasn't going anywhere.

ROXANNE. Oh alright, it's true, it's true. But that's over. I walked away from all that.

BAGGAGE. No, you didn't walk away. He pushed you away. You got into a big argument with him over that property in the Everglades.

ROXANNE. Oh, Mickey was such a fool when it came to money. He knew how to make it, but he didn't know how to spend it. First he throws away all our cash on a hundred acres of swampland in Southern Florida. And then he goes into debt to convert it into a ski resort.

MITZI. Oh wow. Moron city.

ROXANNE. Mickey kept saying, "Look, the weather has to change eventually, right?" He really thought that someday it would snow over the Everglades.

MITZI. And you believed him?

ROXANNE. I tried to, but I couldn't. His pals around town started to joke about him. Talk behind his back. And then I did too. Mickey found out and it was all over between us.

BAGGAGE. I knew it. You didn't walk away at all. If you had your way, you'd still be with him.

ROXANNE. It was a glamorous way of life. I wanted glamor. All I had to do was say "Mickey Melinski" and people thought I was glamorous.

MITZI. Strange crowd down there.

BAGGAGE. What would Eliot say if he found out about all this?

ROXANNE. Oh no, no, you mustn't tell him! Don't you see? I came here to get away from all that. I came here to start fresh. To wipe the slate clean.

BAGGAGE. All I have to do is tell Eliot and he'll drop you like a hot air mass.

ROXANNE. Eliot will never believe you. Never.

BAGGAGE. I have a published article and I have a witness. *(He grabs MITZI's arm.)*

ROXANNE. Where?

BAGGAGE. I have Mitzi. Mitzi knows everything. She just heard your whole sordid story.

MITZI. Who, me? No, no, I didn't hear anything.

BAGGAGE. Mitzi heard everything. And I can force her to testify. I can squeeze her until every rotten word squirts out of her.

MITZI. Oh no please, you wouldn't do that.

BAGGAGE. Do you think I'm above violence?

MITZI. I was hoping you were, yes.

BAGGAGE. Well forget it.

MITZI. *(to ROXANNE)* Oh please don't let him do that. I really can't handle anything physical. All I have is Blue Cross and I lost my card and I....

BAGGAGE. Shut up!

ROXANNE. Oh Rick no. Please! Don't you realize how hard I've worked? My whole life has changed since I met Eliot and now you're going to ruin all that? I see now how wrong I was to chase after all that glitter and money. I don't want that anymore. I want to be something I've never been before. I want to be.... naive. I realize now that all my life, unconsciously, that's all I really wanted to be was Mrs. Eliot Iceberg.

MITZI. Oh wow.

ROXANNE. If you tell Eliot about my past, you'll ruin everything.

BAGGAGE. All this time you've been living a lie.

ROXANNE. Yes, but it was such a nice lie, a warm friendly lie. It hasn't hurt anyone.

BAGGAGE. All I have to do is tell Eliot and you'll be out. Then I'll become the new executive assistant. Yuh, me. Rick Baggage.

ROXANNE. Don't you see it won't work. Eliot loves me. He's overflowing with love for me. He's possessed with love for me. If he finds out about me and Mickey, you'll destroy him. He'll quit weather! That's what he'll do. He'll quit the Service. The President will replace him and the new director will hire his own man. And then where will you be?

BAGGAGE. I'll have to take that chance. I'm going to call Eliot in Illinois. *(He releases MITZI's arm.)*

ROXANNE. No, Baggage, no! You don't have to. Don't you see? I'm only in this job so that I can be close to Eliot. As soon as he asks me to marry him, I'll quit and you can step in. I'll recommend you. He'll promote you on the spot.

BAGGAGE. How do I know I can trust you?

ROXANNE. I don't care about this job. I only care about Eliot. You can always expose me later if I don't keep my promise. But if you do it my way, there'll be no scandal and no mess. You'll get what you want and I'll get what I want.

MITZI. Sounds good. I'll go for coffee.

BAGGAGE. Wait right there. Alright, Roxanne. I'll play along. But if you make one wrong move .... I have twenty-five photocopies of the Carp article in safe deposit boxes all over Washington.

ROXANNE. You can trust me.

BAGGAGE. Yes, I believe I can. Rick Baggage never makes a mistake.

ROXANNE. You'd better get back to your desk now.

BAGGAGE. *(as he leaves)* I'll have my eye on you.

ROXANNE. I won't disappoint you. And Rick....

BAGGAGE. Yes?

ROXANNE. Thanks. I know I can trust you. *(He leaves.)* I don't think I can trust him.

MITZI. Can I leave now?

ROXANNE. Mitzi, you have to promise me never to tell

Eliot about this.

MITZI. Oh Roxanne, why do you have to make me do that?

ROXANNE. You have to promise.

MITZI. But Eliot is always asking me questions and he's always so worried about the reputation of the Service.

ROXANNE. What about my reputation?

MITZI. Well I can't lie to him.

ROXANNE. Why does he have to know that I'm a woman with a past? Why? Why?

MITZI. Gee, I don't know, Roxanne.

ROXANNE. I'm not asking you to do very much. Just don't tell Eliot and stay away from Baggage for awhile, until I can take care of him.

MITZI. Well what if Eliot asks me something. I can't lie to him.

ROXANNE. Mitzi, come closer. I want to have a talk with you — woman to woman. I want you to forget that you're a silly little clerk-typist and that I'm a talented executive on the move. I want you to forget that I've forgotten more about life than you'll ever know. I want you to forget that my index finger could stop traffic, and your whole body couldn't bring in a sailor out of the rain. I want you to think of me as .... just another woman. Could you do that?

MITZI. Sure, Roxanne.

ROXANNE. Because you see, that's all I really am. Just another woman whose found the love that can make her life worthwhile. A rich, deep, satisfying love that flies above the highest clouds, that pierces the strongest winds, that shines through the darkest rain. A love as pure and strong as our entire national weather system. Have you ever felt a love like that Mitzi?

MITZI. Not really, no.

ROXANNE. Well I hope that someday you do. But right now it's all I have and I just can't let anyone take it away from me. You wouldn't want to take it away from me, would you Mitzi?

MITZI. Well, no, but....

ROXANNE. I knew you wouldn't. And just to show you the kind of executive I am, I'm going to go back on what I said before about your silly little office party. You can go ahead and have it, starting at three o'clock.

MITZI. I can't sell out Eliot, just for an office party.

ROXANNE. Oh Mitzi, Mitzi, Mitzi. You're being too hard on yourself. I'm letting you have this party because I have to do what I think is right. And I know you're a good girl, and you'll do the same.

MITZI. Uhuh.

ROXANNE. I'm so glad we understand each other. And now if you'll excuse me....

(The phone rings.)

MITZI. *(Answers phone.)* National Weather Service. *(She listens, then speaks to ROXANNE.)* It's the Florida office returning your call.

ROXANNE. Thank you. *(She takes the phone. MITZI does not move.)* Uhh Mitzi, don't you think it's possible that somewhere in this building there are eggs just waiting to be deviled?

MITZI. Oh. Yuh sure. *(Begins to leave.)*

ROXANNE. Thank you.

MITZI. Boy, creep city. *(She is gone.)*

ROXANNE. *(into the phone)* I'm not in the mood for excuses so you'd better have the right answer. Did you do what I told you to do? *(pause)* And was it taken care of? *(pause)* Good. Now clear the building, shut out the lights, lock the door, and don't let anyone hear from you ever again.

BLACKOUT

Scene 2

ELIOT and MITZI. ELIOT holds a computer printout.

ELIOT. Fourteen inches of snow! With drifts up to two feet! Isn't that terrific?

MITZI. Yes Eliot.

ELIOT. Isn't that wonderful?

MITZI. Yes Eliot.

ELIOT. Aren't you excited?

MITZI. I'm excited, Eliot.

ELIOT. Don't you realize what this says? *(Shows the printout to MITZI.)* This says that it's snowing over the Everglades. Aren't you excited?

MITZI. Do I look like a snow bunny?

ELIOT. No.

MITZI. Is there a tall blonde guy named Sven waiting outside to take me skiing?

ELIOT. No.

MITZI. Then how excited can I get?

ELIOT. I have to go there.

MITZI. Where?

ELIOT. To Florida.

MITZI. You don't want to go to Florida. It's snowing there.

ELIOT. I want to bury my feet in the snow! I want to taste the moisture. I want to feel the wind rush through my hair!

MITZI. I don't think you need me for those things. Can I go back to my desk?

ELIOT. And most of all I want to bring Roxanne there. I want to see Roxanne in the Everglades with a snowflake on each cheek. OH ROXANNE!

MITZI. Oh Eliot....

ELIOT. I need Roxanne. Why can't you find her?

MITZI. I called her apartment. There's no one home.

ELIOT. How can that be? What if there's something wrong? What if she's been kidnapped? Call the police.

MITZI. The police don't know anything.

ELIOT. And what about the Florida office? They don't answer the phone either. I'm starting to get worried about those people. I can't go down there and make an inspection unless they're on the job.

MITZI. What are you going to find out from an inspection? Snow is white? You have problems up here, Eliot.

ELIOT. This is a miracle. This is science. This is hstory.

MITZI. This is stupid. It's a bunch of snow. You sit in it, you get wet, and then you go back inside. That's what snow is.

ELIOT. Call back the local police in Miami and insist that they investigate.

MITZI. Yes Eliot.

ELIOT. And while you're at it, call Baggage. We're gonna get some headlines on this. We're gonna put the weather in the news. We're gonna put the weather up in lights.

MITZI. Eliot, look. I don't think we should press too hard on finding Roxanne, you know what I mean?

ELIOT. What are you talking about?

MITZI. Well I'm sure she'll turn up. And if she doesn't, well there's no point in us finding out what we don't need to know. You know?

ELIOT. No I don't.

MITZI. Well, let's not have the police checking into Roxanne, okay? They'll start asking a lot of questions about her and well .... you know how embarrassing these things get....

ELIOT. Mitzi, I don't know what you're blabbering about. I want answers and I want them now. Go get Baggage.

MITZI. Yes Eliot. *(She leaves.)*

ELIOT. This thing is big. This thing is really big. And we're gonna make it even bigger. It's gonna be big. It's gonna be huge. It's gonna be colossal. It's gonna be .... well, big. That's what it's gonna be. Big.

(MITZI brings in BAGGAGE.)

BAGGAGE. Rick Baggage here.

ELIOT. Sit down, Baggage. *(BAGGAGE sits down.)* Baggage, I hate everything you stand for.

BAGGAGE. I don't stand for anything.

ELIOT. I hate that too. I hate everything about you. Your very presence disgusts me.

BAGGAGE. Does this mean I don't get my promotion?

ELIOT. I can't even look at you. Just the fact that we both drink from the same water cooler makes me sick. *(to MITZI)* I want a new water cooler. Write that down.

MITZI. Yes Eliot.

ELIOT. Do you hear me? Sick.

BAGGAGE. I know why you promote other people over me. It's because they're competent, isn't it. Competence always impresses people. Well who needs it. That's what I say. Rick Baggage doesn't need competence to succeed. I never did and I never will. I'll settle for lies and deception any day.

ELIOT. You think you're holding all the cards, don't you Baggage.

MITZI. Eliot, what am I doing here?

ELIOT. Take notes.

MITZI. Why?

BAGGAGE. Your two-bit boss wants to publish his memoirs. Isn't that it, Iceberg?

ELIOT. So what if it is. "The Education of a Weatherman — My Life in the Clouds."

BAGGAGE. You won't sell two copies of it without a dirty picture on the cover. Like you naked, holding a wind vane.

ELIOT. Shut your filthy mouth. You think just because the President made me hire you, that makes you special.

BAGGAGE. Yeah, that's right. Rick Baggage always knows the score.

ELIOT. I curse the day I hired you. Why does the President need you? Why does he need to wade through the quicksand of degradation? Why does he need to swim through the sewers of filth? Why does he need to bathe his body in the cesspool of corruption?

BAGGAGE. Because he needs votes in New Jersey, that's why. Who do you think pushes the buttons for him? Yuh, that's right. Rick Baggage. You think you can carry Monmouth County with honesty? What a joke. It doesn't take honesty. It takes Rick Baggage.

MITZI. Eliot, what are you talking to him for?

ELIOT. Oh the shame. I knew it. I knew it had to be something like this. Oh the shame!

BAGGAGE. Oh can it, Iceberg. Get to the point. You must want something filthy from me, otherwise you wouldn't be letting me filthy your filthy carpet.

ELIOT. Yes. Yes and I regret it already, but I have no choice. I can't get a bigger budget unless I get the weather in the news. And the only way to do that is to exaggerate. All I need is a press release that bends the facts a little. Something that'll make the storm in Florida look just a little worse than it really is. Just enough so that it becomes a national story and I can get my name in the papers.

MITZI. Eliot, what are you doing?

BAGGAGE. And you want me to hype it up, is that the idea?

ELIOT. You're the only one I could ever get to do this. I can't ask any of the career professionals to fudge instrument readings. They'd never do it.

BAGGAGE. But you know I would, for the right price.

ELIOT. Yes, that's right. If it works out, you'll get your promotion.

MITZI. Oh Eliot....

BAGGAGE. Okay, Iceberg. You got a deal. You'll get your story. *(He starts to leave.)*

ELIOT. But don't go too far with this. I mean it's alright to say that the entire Southeast may be wiped out, but don't cause any panic. Just say that people should, well, they should definitely take in their lawn furniture.

BAGGAGE. Listen, the fix is in. No problem. Rick Baggage never makes a mistake.

ELIOT. Alright, get out of here. *(MITZI escorts BAG-GAGE out.)* Oh my God. What have I done?

MITZI. *(Reenters.)* Congratulations. The weather is in the news. *(She hands him a newspaper clipping.)*

ELIOT. Already? Where's my name? Where's my name?

MITZI. Your name was not considered relevant. It's about some guy named Melinski who had built his own ski resort in the Everglades. Before there was any storm, he had already built a ski resort.

ELIOT. You mean water skiing?

MITZI. No, snow skiing. You know, like downhill?

ELIOT. There aren't any hills in the Everglades.

MITZI. He built a six thousand foot incline — Mount Melinski. He's gonna make a fortune. It's the only place in the country to go skiing in August. All the networks went down there to interview him.

ELIOT. To interview him? Him? *(He crumples the clipping and throws it aside.)* What about me? When is it my turn? I need some appreciation.

MITZI. I appreciate you, Eliot.

ELIOT. I need some gratification.

MITZI. I gratify you. I mean you gratify me. I feel gratified.

ELIOT. I need more. I need .... I need inner peace.

MITZI. Eliot, you're dealing with a clerk-typist.

ELIOT. It just isn't fair.

MITZI. Well what am I supposed to do? I'm sorry you're not in the newspaper. I'm sorry you're not on television. What do you expect me to do? You want me to lie for you too?

ELIOT. I need Roxanne!

MITZI. Ahh yes. Back to basics.

ELIOT. Where is Roxanne?

MITZI. I give up. Where?

ELIOT. That's what I asked you. Where is Roxanne?

MITZI. She isn't answering her phone.

ELIOT. Send somebody to her apartment.

MITZI. Eliot, I don't want to look for Roxanne.

ELIOT. What are you talking about?

MITZI. How well do you know her?

ELIOT. That's none of your business.

MITZI. I don't mean that way. I just mean she's only been in Washington for a few weeks and you've given her all this responsibility. Do you know where she came from?

ELIOT. She came from Ohio and I don't like the tone of these questions.

MITZI. Well maybe it would be a good idea if you checked out some of her job references before we start looking for her.

ELIOT. Mitzi you are overstepping your position and I don't like it.

MITZI. Well I'm only doing it to protect you.

ELIOT. If you think you can evade your responsibility by impugning Roxanne's reputation, then you are sorely mistaken.

MITZI. I just don't want to see you get hurt.

ELIOT. If I hear one more word from you about Roxanne, you can consider yourself on probation.

MITZI. Yes Eliot.

ELIOT. Now instead of spreading vile rumors about Roxanne's integrity, you should be trying to find her. Where is she?

MITZI. I don't know.

ELIOT. Well why can't you find out?

MITZI. Because I don't know where to look.

ELIOT. That is not a dynamic answer, Mitzi. When I ask questions I expect dynamic answers. Now find her.

MITZI. How about if I look up her mother in the phone book?

ELIOT. And what about the people in the Florida office? Where are they?

MITZI. In Florida, right?

ELIOT. No they're not.

MITZI. Well, that's two questions I missed today.

(The phone rings offstage.)

ELIOT. There is still no one in the Florida office answering the phone. Why isn't anybody answering their phones today?

MITZI. Eliot, the problem isn't in Florida. The problem is here. You're going to get into big trouble with that press release. How could you trust Baggage to do that?

ELIOT. It had to be done. And I will not have my

decisions questioned.

MITZI. Eliot, I'm trying to help you. Doesn't that mean anything to you?

ELIOT. You are now on probation.

MITZI. But Eliot....

ELIOT. Go answer the phone. *(MITZI starts to leave.)* Come back here.

MITZI. What is it?

ELIOT. Call the local police in Florida again and insist that they check out the building. And if that doesn't work, call the FBI. I'm gonna get to the bottom of this.

MITZI. I'll help you get right to the bottom, Eliot. *(She leaves.)*

ELIOT. Who cares about a ski resort in the Everglades? Who cares about skiing? They should be worried about the blizzard. They should be worried about the repercussions. They should be worried about the fate of the nation.

MITZI. *(entering)* You just got a telegram about the fate of the nation.

ELIOT. From who?

MITZI. The United Farmers of Southeast North Carolina.

ELIOT. I never heard of them.

MITZI. They just formed ten minutes ago. They're coming here in a tractor.

ELIOT. Why?

MITZI. To level the building.

ELIOT. Just because of a little snow?

MITZI. Our press release said there was no future in farming. The fields will be permanently frozen.

ELIOT. Get Baggage in here.

MITZI. *(Goes to the doorway and calls.)* BAGGAGE!

(BAGGAGE enters from the other direction.)

BAGGAGE. Rick Baggage here.

ELIOT. Baggage, what is the meaning of this?

BAGGAGE. The meaning of what?

MITZI. Now you two boys have a nice talk and I'll go get some Oreos and milk. *(She starts to leave.)*

ELIOT. Stay where you are. Baggage, what is the meaning of this?

BAGGAGE. What is the meaning of what?

MITZI. He doesn't know the meaning, Eliot.

ELIOT. He'd better know the meaning.

MITZI. Why don't I go out and get the meaning and bring it back here with the Oreos.

ELIOT. You stay here. Baggage, what are you putting in these press releases?

BAGGAGE. I'm writing about the storm.

ELIOT. You weren't supposed to say that the entire Southeast would be blown off the map.

BAGGAGE. You told me to exaggerate.

ELIOT. I said exaggerate a little.

BAGGAGE. You told me to jazz it up. You said we wanted lots of press.

(The phone begins ringing offstage.)

ELIOT. You were supposed to say there was a little snow. You weren't supposed to say it was a new ice age.

BAGGAGE. Well you didn't tell me you were gonna be so picky about it.

MITZI. You guys want milk or what?

ELIOT. Will you answer the phone please? *(MITZI leaves.)*

ELIOT. Frozen fields? Those farmers will turn me into a scarecrow. And it's all your fault. Well you can forget about that promotion, Baggage. You can forget about it.

BAGGAGE. What did you say? Rick Baggage does not get double-crossed by anyone. You better change your mind, Eliot, or you're in big trouble.

MITZI. *(Enters.)* The FBI is here.

ELIOT. The FBI?

MITZI. Yes. The FBI. You wanted them to be called in, didn't you?

ELIOT. The FBI?

MITZI. Well not the whole FBI. I could only fit two agents in the waiting room. The rest of them are outside.

ELIOT. What are they doing here so fast?

MITZI. They want to talk to you about this Melinski guy.

ELIOT. What Melinski guy?

MITZI. The one who built the ski resort in Florida. They think it's very suspicious, with the snowstorm and everything.

ELIOT. I don't know anything about Melinski. I don't want to talk to the FBI.

MITZI. It's not going to be a real interrogation. They just like to chew gum and point their fingers at people.

What are you worried about?

ELIOT. Tell them I'll see them as soon as I can.

MITZI. Eliot, there's only one magazine out there.

ELIOT. Ask them to take turns.

MITZI. *(exiting)* I don't think they like to do that.

ELIOT. I'll see them as soon as I can.

BAGGAGE. You'd better change your mind about that promotion, Eliot.

ELIOT. Baggage, get out of here.

BAGGAGE. Are you telling me to leave your office?

ELIOT. Leave my office.

BAGGAGE. I don't think I heard that.

MITZI. *(Enters.)* Senator Orbit's key aide is in the other waiting room.

ELIOT. Which key aide? What's his name?

MITZI. He said he doesn't have a name. He's the Senator's key aide. That's all he kept saying. He's the key aide.

ELIOT. I can't see him now.

MITZI. He wants an explanation for the storm. He's getting complaints.

ELIOT. I don't have an explanation.

MITZI. Well the FBI is reading the only magazine. What am I supposed to tell him?

ELIOT. The Senator wants to embarrass me. It's a deliberate attempt to embarrass me. We finally make the news. We finally get the weather in the news and get a little hard-earned notoriety, and they're trying to cut us down. And do you know why? Do you know why?

MITZI. No. Why?

ELIOT. It's because Senator Orbit is stupid, ignorant,

and short-sighted.

MITZI. Well, I'll tell him that, but he's still gonna want a magazine. *(She exits.)*

BAGGAGE. I want that promotion, Eliot.

ELIOT. Baggage, we do not have anymore time for this.

BAGGAGE. I know why you don't have anymore time. It's because you're jealous.

ELIOT. Jealous?

BAGGAGE. You're jealous of me. You know I have the stuff to make a much better director than you.

ELIOT. Baggage, I have reached the end of my patience with you.

BAGGAGE. I could have been the director. Yuh, me. Rick Baggage. I could have been the director. But the President picked you. And do you know why? I'll tell you why. The President chose you just because I didn't know anything about meterology. That's the only reason he chose you.

ELIOT. That's enough.

BAGGAGE. You let Roxanne take over the whole service.

ELIOT. Roxanne is a dedicated public servant. If she were here now, she'd fire you.

BAGGAGE. But she isn't here, is she.

MITZI. *(Enters.)* The FBI wants to see you immediately.

ELIOT. Don't you ever have any good news?

MITZI. *(Tosses a small package onto ELIOT's desk.)* Your bow tie is back from the cleaners.

ELIOT. Why now? Why does it have to be now?

MITZI. I don't know. They finished cleaning it so they

figured they'd bring it over. You want me to send it back?

ELIOT. No! Why does the FBI have to see me now?

MITZI. They just got word from their office. A person fitting Roxanne's description was seen last night on a midnight flight to Miami.

BAGGAGE. Aha! I was right. I knew it!

ELIOT. Roxanne? A midnight flight? Miami? What does this mean?

MITZI. I tried to warn you.

ELIOT. Go back to your desk. *(MITZI exits.)*

BAGGAGE. It means that Roxanne is in the Everglades with Melinski. Right now.

ELIOT. Melinski with the ski resort? She doesn't even know him.

BAGGAGE. Oh, she knows him alright. She knew him before she came here. She's from Florida, you idiot. Melinski was a mobster. She was his woman.

ELIOT. She's from Ohio.

BAGGAGE. She's a tramp from the swamp. You know what they call a tramp from the swamp in Florida? A swamp tramp. Look at this article. *(BAGGAGE hands ELIOT the newspaper clipping from the Sarasota Carp. ELIOT reads it.)* Melinski planted Roxanne here. All she had to do was get close to you and the whole weather bureau opened up to her. She fixed it so it would snow in the Everglades and Melinski would make a fortune. They're in his ski lodge in Florida right now, toasting each other's marshmallows.

ELIOT. Roxanne? That kind of a woman?

BAGGAGE. Yes, Eliot. That kind of a woman.

ELIOT. She was so good to me. So true to me. So sweet to me.

BAGGAGE. All lies.

ELIOT. No, it's impossible. Even if I believed the garbage in this article, which I don't, no one can create weather. A little cloud-seeding maybe, but a blizzard? Even Roxanne can not make it snow over the Everglades. No one would believe that. Absolutely no one would believe that.

MITZI. *(entering)* The FBI believes that Roxanne made it snow over the Everglades.

ELIOT. On what basis?

MITZI. They've established a connection between Roxanne and Melinski. They want to talk to you about it right now.

(We hear the FBI agents banging on the door.)

ELIOT. I can't talk to them.

MITZI. What am I supposed to tell them? They finished the magazine. They want to come in.

(We hear banging at the other door.)

MITZI. The key aide wants to come in too. What am I supposed to do?

BAGGAGE. You don't know anything about the weather, Eliot. Everything you've always believed is wrong.

(We hear banging on two doors. It continues intermittently through the rest of the scene.)

ELIOT. Shut up, Baggage. Just shut up.

BAGGAGE. What a loser. Gimme a call when you're ready to throw in the washcloth. Don't forget the name. It's Rick Baggage.

ELIOT. I said shut up! *(BAGGAGE laughs and exits.)*

MITZI. If only you had a few more magazines, I'd have something to work with.

ELIOT. And you shut up too. Why didn't you warn me about this woman?

MITZI. I did warn you. You wouldn't listen.

ELIOT. Why did you let me hire her?

MITZI. I didn't let you hire her. You hired her. I'm the secretary.

ELIOT. You didn't even check her job references.

MITZI. *You're* supposed to check her job references.

ELIOT. Well you're supposed to remind me.

MITZI. What was I supposed to do?

ELIOT. Well you didn't have to let me fall in love with her.

MITZI. You didn't ask me for permission.

ELIOT. If you were doing your filing correctly, this wouldn't have happened.

MITZI. What are you talking about?

ELIOT. This whole thing is your fault. It's all your fault.

(The phone rings.)

MITZI. Well what was I supposed to do?

ELIOT. You were supposed to be dynamic. I hired you to be dynamic.

MITZI. *(answering the phone)* National Weather Service, God damn it.

ELIOT. How could this happen?

MITZI. It's the White House.

ELIOT. The White House?

MITZI. They say the President wants to talk to which-ever idiot is in charge up here.

ELIOT. Well that does it. I'm not gonna get yelled at. *(He begins to gather things and pack them into his attache case.)*

MITZI. Eliot, the President is on hold.

ELIOT. I'm not gonna be the one they find here. I know that much.

MITZI. What are you doing?

ELIOT. You're in charge *(He makes for the door.)*

MITZI. Where are you going?

ELIOT. Out.

MITZI. What am I supposed to do?

ELIOT. You're now the acting director. Best of luck. *(He leaves.)*

MITZI. Eliot! The FBI is outside, Eliot. I can't stand people with ID cards. Eliot! Come back here! I don't know how she made it snow. What am I supposed to tell them?

(more banging on the doors)

MITZI. I don't know. Don't you hear me? I don't know!

BLACKOUT

ACT II

Scene 1

MITZI, now dressed as a tour guide, leads a couple, LEONARD and NORMA, onstage. They are tired.

MITZI. And so these millions of dollars worth of instruments enable us to predict the weather in such strange and faraway places as Caribou, Maine and Climax, Nevada. Unfortunately, we are totally unable to predict the weather in such places as Philadelphia, Cleveland, or anyplace else where there are actually people living. *(Motions to indicate the room.)* We are now in the office of our acting Executive Director, Richard C. Baggage. This is the Executive Director's chair. There's no one in that chair right now because Mr. Baggage is goofing off somewhere at the taxpayers' expense, throwing empty gum wrappers into baby carriages, squirting warm beer into the faces of widows and orphans, and showing his basic contempt for society. *(Motions to desk.)* This is the Executive Director's pen and this is the Executive Director's pencil. Of course here at the National Weather Service, we like to refer to them together as the Executive Director's pen and pencil.

NORMA. *(to LEONARD)* How much longer is this going to go on?

LEONARD. You wanted to take the tour so we're going to take the tour.

MITZI. This is the director's leather-covered appointment calendar. He uses it to make appointments with people who are covered with leather.

NORMA. *(to LEONARD)* Where are my pills? Did you hide them again?

MITZI. This brings us to the midpoint of our special fourteen-hour tour of the National Weather Service. During the intermission, ice cream and other tasty treats are available at the Partly Cloudy Soda Fountain. After a refreshing drink, feel free to browse in our National Weather Service Gift Shop. Today's special is a three-hour recording of snow falling. *(MITZI slumps into a chair. NORMA blows her nose.)*

LEONARD. Look, I'm sorry you caught a cold upstairs in the artificial ice storm, but this whole thing was your idea.

NORMA. I never felt so tired before I met you, Leonard. I never felt so weary.

LEONARD. Oh you revolt me. It's my fault that you feel so tired? Why don't you quit those sky diving lessons?

NORMA. I have to learn sky diving. There are many times when we're up in a plane together and I just feel that I need to get away from you. *(They both sit down and try to sleep.)*

(BAGGAGE enters and sees MITZI goofing off.)

BAGGAGE. We're not paying you a salary to test out the chairs, you know.

MITZI. This is my coffee break.

BAGGAGE. If you want to keep your job, sweetheart, you'll learn to take your coffee break before you come to work. Now get up and sell those buttons and T-shirts.

MITZI. You'll never get away with this, Baggage. Selling souvenirs you didn't pay for. Using government property for personal profit.

BAGGAGE. You're just jealous because I thought of it first.

MITZI. What would Eliot say if he saw this?

BAGGAGE. Oh, that fool wouldn't even know what was happening. He was in this office for six months and he never made himself a dime. He felt guilty about drawing a salary. I've been acting director for three days and I just put a down payment on a brand new six-bedroom in Georgetown. I'm in the money, baby, and I'm gonna make the most of it. Fancy cars, fancy jewelry, monogrammed Kleenex. The whole number.

MITZI. I don't believe this. I was better off with Eliot.

BAGGAGE. *(raising his pant legs)* Look at these socks. Pure velvet. They itch like hell, but it's worth it. That hot young regulation officer from the Interstate Commerce Commission wouldn't even spit on me before this. But wait until she sees my new socks.

MITZI. Yuh, she'll certainly spit on you then, I'll bet.

BAGGAGE. No, she'll let me spit on her and she'll love it. I'm gonna get her right in her truck routes.

MITZI. Eliot would never lower himself to this. He was a little stupid, but at least he was a nice guy.

BAGGAGE. Yuh, well you know what they say about nice guys.

MITZI. They finish last?

BAGGAGE. No, they make you feel guilty. Well I had it with that. No nice boy is ever gonna make me feel guilty again. Sure, sure, I know I'm a crumb. But I like it. I like being a crumb.

MITZI. Well I don't. And as soon as I can figure out a way to get out of this, I'm going to set fire to your socks and run like hell.

BAGGAGE. Oh yeah? Well in the meantime, I want you hustling those souvenirs. Now get on it!

MITZI. Oh lay off. You'll make a hundred thousand this week easy.

BAGGAGE. You think we're gonna be satisfied with a lousy hundred thousand bucks? Hahh! That's nothing. We got bigger plans.

MITZI. What do you mean, we. Whose "we?"

BAGGAGE. Who do you think dimples? Me and Roxanne. We're gonna clean up. This storm is just the beginning.

MITZI. What are you talking about? You didn't tell me you were in on the storm.

BAGGAGE. Who says I was, lamb chop. But I know a good thing when I see it. There's money in weather, Mitzi. And why shouldn't I get my share?

MITZI. The ski resort? They already have that set up. What do you need you for?

BAGGAGE. Because I'm on the inside. Roxanne's name has been in all the papers. She can't get back in here. But I'm in the driver's seat and they know it. If they want the right buttons pushed, they have to come to me.

MITZI.   Are you telling me that you know how she made it snow?

BAGGAGE.   Not yet. But she and Melinski have to tell me sooner or later. They can't get what they want without me.

MITZI.   But why are you doing this? There couldn't be that much money in a lousy ski lodge.

BAGGAGE.   The money isn't in the ski resort, girlie. The money is in my concept, my design, my plan. If Roxanne can do snowstorms, she can do a lot more.

MITZI.   Your plan?

BAGGAGE.   Yuh, that's right. My plan.

MITZI.   And what plan is that?

BAGGAGE.   Why should I tell you? Why should I unclothe my genius? Why should I tell you about the greatest plan that's ever been planned in the history of planning?

MITZI.   Well, if you don't want to....

BAGGAGE.   Oh alright. You forced it out of me. My plan is called N.D.I.

MITZI.   N.D.I.?

BAGGAGE.   Natural Disasters Incorporated. We'll do everything — floods, hurricanes, earthquakes, tidal waves, volcanic eruptions. Anything that causes massive damage and personal injury.

MITZI.   That's terrible.

BAGGAGE.   Exactly. Our motto is — "If it's rotten, we do it."

MITZI.   Roxanne knows how to make earthquakes?

BAGGAGE.   She'll learn. She did the storm, didn't she?

MITZI. I don't believe this. Baggage, you're talking about destruction of entire cities and towns. The loss of human lives.

BAGGAGE. Well you can't make an omelette without breaking eggs.

MITZI. This is insane. I knew you always wanted to be a jerk. I didn't think you were going to be perverted about it. What are you doing this for?

BAGGAGE. For the money, why else? There's a fortune here. First there's the insurance. Everybody's got disaster insurance. We provide the disaster, they collect, and we split it fifty-fifty. Then there's real estate development. Suppose somebody wants to build a shopping mall, but he can't acquire enough land. We just whip up a tornado and that scares away all the old property owners. They sell out for a song.

MITZI. That's grand larceny.

BAGGAGE. Yuh, isn't it great? Then there's my favorite. Full scale destruction of the democratic process. Suppose some county executive is stuck with opposition from a few crummy townships way out in the sticks. The old way to knock them off was to accidentally dump their voting machines off the side of a cliff.

MITZI. You mean you would actually do that?

BAGGAGE. Not that often. It cost too much to rent the truck. But now we don't have to. All we have to do is create a small earthquake in the right place and ten thousand voters will pack up and move out of the county.

MITZI. Baggage, this is ridiculous. You don't have to destroy people's lives to get ahead. You're the acting director of the National Weather Service. You're making a top salary and you have a friend in the White House. What more could you want?

BAGGAGE. I want respect, that's what I want.

MITZI. You think you'll be respected for breaking the law?

BAGGAGE. Well I'm not going back to Jersey as some air-headed bureaucrat. I don't push pencils for nobody. I'm Rick Baggage. You hear me? Rick Baggage. And someday there'll be statues of me all over Jersey City. And children will ask their parents, "Who was that man?" And they'll all say, "That was Rick Baggage. He changed the meaning of the word extortion."

MITZI. Oh my God.....

BAGGAGE. "Rick Baggage discovered the frontier of slime. And he crossed it."

MITZI. You can't do this.

BAGGAGE. Sure we can. If Roxanne could create a snowstorm in Florida, then we can figure out how to do anything. Natural Disasters, Inc. It brings tears to my eyes. It's so beautiful, I can't stand it.

MITZI. What am I doing here?

BAGGAGE. Alright, can the blabber. Get back to work. Make me some money. We need some front-end cash to finance the equipment. Disasters don't come cheap, you know. We already got an order to flood three towns in Indiana. I can't keep our customers waiting. Get on it!

MITZI. I have to work every day to create a tidal wave in Indiana? I don't need this. Four-twenty an hour and I'm supposed to do floods? And who do you think you are destroying people's property? Well? Who do you think you are?

BAGGAGE. I'm Rick Ba....

MITZI. Oh shut up! Who wants to listen to you. I have to listen to this? I have to listen all day long to a crooked ward healer from New Jersey? What is this? Wisdom from Bayonne? I don't need this. I came here to type letters, not drown children. I am not going to be part of any crooked real estate deal or any insurance swindle. How did you get to be this way, Baggage? How did you get to be such a creep? Such an immoral twirp? How did you get to be such a piece of crud?

BAGGAGE. Anyone can fall in with the wrong crowd.

MITZI. Do you expect me to help you destroy half of Indiana?

BAGGAGE. Well all I....

MITZI. Didn't I tell you to shut up?

BAGGAGE. Yuh, that is what you said....

MITZI. Then shut up! I don't need this! You thought I'd put up with anything, didn't you. Well this is where I get off. This far and no further. I gave up a nice job at the National Science Foundation typing labels on dirt. I figured this would be more interesting. Well forget it. I don't need this. I quit!

BAGGAGE. Now wait a minute, babyface. I can't let you walk out of here just like that. You know too much. You'll blab this all over town.

MITZI. You can't stop me, Baggage.

BAGGAGE. I can't, huh? Well you try it. I'll give you a recommendation so bad you'll be in charge of disinfectant at the Washington Monument. I'll say you were fired from this job for incompetence.

MITZI. You can't do that. I'll appeal to Civil Service.

BAGGAGE. I got friends there too, babyface. You'll never work in this town again.

MITZI. You can't do this to me.

BAGGAGE. Oh yeah? And what are you going to do about it?

MITZI. If Roxanne figured out a way to start that storm then I can figure out a way to stop it.

BAGGAGE. You end the storm? Don't make me laugh. *(He laughs.)* I told you not to make me laugh.

MITZI. Oh can it. If I can stop the snowstorm in Florida, then your whole plan isn't worth a frozen cent.

BAGGAGE. Oh yeah? Well I got nothing to worry about. Because even if you knew how to end the storm, you haven't got the guts to do it. You know what they call a secretary with no guts in New Jersey? A gutless New Jersey secretary. And you're no better. Now get off your high pressure area and sell those souvenirs.

MITZI. Alright, Baggage. I'll play along for awhile. But you're headed for a fall.

BAGGAGE. Didn't I tell you to move those souvenirs?

MITZI. *(indicating NORMA and LEONARD)* They're exhausted. They can't walk to the Gift Shop.

BAGGAGE. Bring the Gift Shop to them, damn it. Sell her one of those T-shirts that say "Warm Front." They love that. Anything filthy. That's what people like nowadays. Now go downstairs and bring that stuff up here.

MITZI. I'm tired.

BAGGAGE. I said move.

MITZI. Go shine your socks. *(BAGGAGE pushes MITZI off. They are both gone.)*

LEONARD. Where am I going? Where is society going?

Where am I going in society?

NORMA. Could you look for my maroon pills please?

LEONARD. Why am I so dissatisfied with our marriage? It's not that I dislike you.

NORMA. Thank you, Leonard. As long as you find the pills, I won't dislike you either.

LEONARD. But why are we so cranky? Why are we so miserable?

NORMA. I don't know, Leonard. Our marriage was fine until we went on vacation. I don't suppose there are any drugstores in this City?

LEONARD. That's it. It isn't our marriage. It's this tour. It's this God damned tour!

NORMA. What are you talking about?

LEONARD. I don't hate you at all, Norma. I love you! *(He hugs her.)* The only thing I hate now ... is the National Weather Service.

NORMA. The National Weather Service? Yeah. Yeah, I hate them too. Bunch of animals. How dare they make us walk around this stupid ass building for fourteen hours.

LEONARD. What kind of government agency would make two adults who had never done anything wrong in their lives stand through a forty-five minute slide show on the Gulf Stream?

NORMA. And then two hours standing in an artificial cloud? My sinuses are forming a militia.

(MITZI and BAGGAGE return. MITZI drops all of her boxes on the floor.)

LEONARD. Well I'm not going to take this sitting down.

Leonard Mouth is a man of action.

BAGGAGE. Did these people pay in advance?

MITZI. Yes, Baggage.

BAGGAGE. Quick! Give me the money. *(She hands him the money. He stuffs it into his coat pocket.)*

LEONARD. I saw that, you crumb!

BAGGAGE. Excuse me?

LEONARD. You just pocketed the admission money.

NORMA. You crumb!

LEONARD. You're stealing from the American people.

BAGGAGE. So what. You gonna make something out of it?

NORMA. You crumb!

LEONARD. We demand our two hundred dollars back.

NORMA. Yeah, that's right. I'm tired of being a smiling tourist all day long. I'm always nasty at home. Why shouldn't I be nasty when I'm on vacation? Fork it over.

BAGGAGE. Not on your life.

MITZI. Oh give them back their money, Baggage.

BAGGAGE. And you stay out of this.

MITZI. If they didn't like the tour you have to give them back the two hundred dollars. It's a money back guarantee.

BAGGAGE. I didn't sign anything. And I told you to stay out of this.

MITZI. *(throwing off her tour guide hat)* Then run your own tour, slime-face. *(She exits.)*

BAGGAGE. *(Starts to follow her.)* Come back here, you.

NORMA. Not so fast, you crumb. Pay up.

LEONARD. Step aside, Norma. *(to BAGGAGE)* You're not just dealing with some stupid nobody, you know.

BAGGAGE. Gee, I thought I was. *(LEONARD hands BAGGAGE a business card. BAGGAGE reads.)* "Leonard Mouth. Attorney at Law. Specializing in Negligance."

LEONARD. You'll never get away with this, you crumb.

BAGGAGE. Mr. Crumb to you.

LEONARD. As soon as I leave here, I'm filing a writ.

BAGGAGE. You couldn't file your nails, you idiot. Who are they going to believe? A backwoods loopholer or the acting director of the National Weather Service? You don't scare me, Mouth.

LEONARD. Oh yeah? Well you can't keep this hidden forever. Who would ever expect this kind of graft? This kind of corruption?

BAGGAGE. Well what kind did you expect?

NORMA. As soon as we get home, I'm reporting you to my travel agent.

BAGGAGE. Oh dry up, bitch. Go eat your pills.

NORMA. You'll never get away with this. Sooner or later, someone will find you out.

BAGGAGE. That's all I need is a few more days of that storm in Florida. As long as the storm holds out, Eliot will be under suspicion and I'll be kept as acting director.

LEONARD. Someone else will find out.

BAGGAGE. No. No one will find out. And if we had a slightly more discrete tour guide, you wouldn't have found out. You don't stand a chance, Mouth. As long as it's snowing in Florida, I'm in the money.

LEONARD. You'll pay for this, Baggage.

BAGGAGE. Not while I have the storm. That storm is my ticket to paradise.

(MITZI reenters, carrying computer printout.)

MITZI. I told you I'd find a way to stop you, Baggage. And now I have.

BAGGAGE. Go drink your correction fluid, dimples.

MITZI. The storm in Florida is over, Baggage. And I was the one who ended it.

BAGGAGE. What are you talking about?

MITZI. Read this, you worm. The storm is over. *(She hands him computer printout. He reads.)* I told you I'd do it and I did it.

BAGGAGE. The storm is over? The storm is over? How can this be?

MITZI. It's easy, once you know how.

BAGGAGE. How did you do this?

MITZI. That's my secret, Baggage. But if I can stop your snowstorm, I can stop your earthquakes or your hurricanes just as easy.

LEONARD. I knew it! I knew justice would prevail!

NORMA. Forget justice. Get the money and let's get out of here.

BAGGAGE. Oh my God....

LEONARD. We've won, Norma. With the storm over, everyone will rush in to investigate. And we can be the first to expose him. We'll be famous. I'd better start drawing up the law suit. *(He takes over BAGGAGE's desk and begins working.)*

NORMA. Leonard, what are you doing?

BAGGAGE. This can't be.

MITZI. Forget about Natural Disasters, Baggage. Forget about it.

LEONARD. What are you going to do now, you worm.

NORMA. *(to LEONARD)* Leonard, I am tired, I am sick, and I am out of my maroon pills and my lavender pills. Why can't we just leave?

LEONARD. It's my responsibility, Norma. I am an officer of the court.

BAGGAGE. There has to be a way to start that storm again.

MITZI. I don't think so, Baggage.

BAGGAGE. If Roxanne did it once, she can do it again.

MITZI. Not while I'm around. You'll excuse us, Baggage. We have to finish the tour.

BAGGAGE. Forget the tour. We have to find Roxanne. Lock the doors and hold all the calls.

LEONARD. I hope you're sentenced to ten thousand years.

NORMA. Yuh, and I hope you go to jail too.

BAGGAGE. And get these people out of here!

MITZI. I'll think about it.

BLACKOUT

Scene 2

*MITZI stands alone inside her supply closet, trying to figure out
what to do next. ROXANNE enters the closet, wearing a
cowboy hat.*

MITZI. This is my supply closet. What are you doing
here?

ROXANNE. Quiet. I'm here in disguise. *(She checks to see if
anyone else is in the closet and then removes the cowboy hat.)*

MITZI. You mean this isn't Dale Evans?

ROXANNE. No one else knows I'm in town. If you tell
antone you saw me, I'll deny everything.

MITZI. Why don't you just leave? That way I won't have
to make up any stories.

ROXANNE. Baggage told me everything. He didn't tell
me you liked to stand alone inside your supply closet, but
that's not important now. Because I know that you were
the one who stopped the storm.

MITZI. Oh yeah? What's it to you?

ROXANNE. Hey. Don't act tough with me, sister. Nobody acts tough with me. Because I'm the toughest.

MITZI. Then what did you come to see me for?

ROXANNE. Because you ruined my plan! *(Pounds her fists
on the wall and cries.)* You ruined everything! I just wanted a

chance to get away from Florida. To get away from the mud, away from the weeds, away from the God damn orange juice all day long. And you ruined it. You ruined it, you ruined it, you ruined it! *(Continues crying.)*

MITZI. Why do you have to create disasters? Can't you find a nice way to make a living? I'm sure there are some pleasant people down there. Suppose I lend you enough money for a bus ticket back to Florida?

ROXANNE. *(immediately regaining her composure)* Back off, Jack. I don't take pity from anyone. Now let's get it all on the table. I know that you know how to do it.

MITZI. Yeah, that's right. I know how to do it. And when I do it, it feels good.

ROXANNE. Yeah? Well .... we can't have you going all over the country undoing our natural disasters. It'll ruin everything. So I'm prepared to make you an offer. We'll give you thirty percent of Natural Disasters Inc. if you promise to keep your hands off.

MITZI. You want to buy me off?

ROXANNE. Keep your voice down.

MITZI. You have no morals whatsoever.

ROXANNE. Sure, I know I'm white trash. So what. Everybody's got to be something, don't they.

MITZI. So you want me to be your partner, is that it?

ROXANNE. There's big money in tragedy. And if you miss it, then you've missed it.

MITZI. I'll think about it.

ROXANNE. I don't have time for deliberation, school girl. Are you in or out?

MITZI. Alright, I'm in. But under one consideration. I want your copy of the plan.

ROXANNE. Why should I give it to you?

MITZI. If I'm your partner, I want to know what you're doing, every step of the way.

ROXANNE. And if I say no?

MITZI. Then the deal is off. You get no more snow in Florida, no floods in Indiana, no nothing. I snap my fingers and your whole number is dead. I want the plan.

ROXANNE. Do you know how much this thing costs to xerox?

MITZI. Give me the plan, Roxanne.

ROXANNE. *(Hands over the plan to MITZI.)* Alright, it's yours. But you'd better not try anything cute. Because I'm the toughest. I was born tough and I'll die tough.

MITZI. I know that, Roxanne.

ROXANNE. Well I want to hear you say it.

MITZI. Say what?

ROXANNE. Say "Roxanne, you're the toughest."

MITZI. Roxanne, you're the toughest.

ROXANNE. That's right. And don't you forget it. *(Puts the cowboy hat back on and leaves the closet.)*

MITZI. Crybaby!

BLACKOUT

Scene 3

ELIOT and MITZI stand downstage.

ELIOT. But I just .... I just don't understand.

MITZI. I've explained it to you three times. This is the plan. It's Baggage's plan for Natural Disasters. Take the plan to Senator Orbit. He'll reinstate you and put Roxanne and Baggage behind bars. This is evidence, Eliot. Take it to Senator Orbit.

ELIOT. But ..... but I just don't understand.

MITZI. There's nothing to understand. Just take this to Orbit's office. He'll realize that none of this was your fault and he'll fix everything up.

ELIOT. But I don't understand.

MITZI. Will you stop saying that.

ELIOT. But how did you get it to stop snowing in Florida?

MITZI. I told you. I didn't get it to stop snowing in Florida. The storm ended and I told Baggage that I did it. He's as stupid as you are and he believed it.

ELIOT. Then who ended the storm?

MITZI. I don't know, Eliot, and I don't care. That's the weather. Who gives a damn about the weather?

ELIOT. I just don't understand.

58

MITZI. I don't have time for you to understand. You're the only one who can do this. That's why I brought you back here. At least Orbit will listen to you. I'm nobody. I couldn't get in to see his tennis instructor. Even the key aide didn't remember me. I gave him a copy of the plan for Natural Disasters, and he laughed. He thought it was very funny that a secretary from the National Weather Service should ask to speak to a U.S. Senator. He laughed at me, Eliot. Do you understand what that feels like?

ELIOT. I don't understand anything anymore.

MITZI. Don't you even care about yourself? Don't you want your job back?

ELIOT. It's no use. I can only think of Roxanne.

MITZI. Eliot, this is not a good time to fall in love again.

ELIOT. Oh Roxanne, I love you.

MITZI. Eliot, she betrayed you.

ELIOT. Yuh, but I liked being betrayed. I liked it. Oh I wish she'd do it again.

MITZI. Eliot, the weather needs you. The weather wants you to take the plan to Senator Orbit. Explain to him that the storm wasn't your idea. It was all Roxanne's fault.

ELIOT. But I can't do that!

MITZI. Why not?

(LEONARD and NORMA enter, arguing about LEONARD's handwritten manuscript, which NORMA waves in the air.)

NORMA. You call this legible?

LEONARD. Yuh, I call it legible.

NORMA. I don't call this legible. *(They argue on, etc.)*

ELIOT. Because ... because ... who are these people?

MITZI. These are the Mouths. This is Leonard Mouth and Norma Mouth.

LEONARD. *(to ELIOT)* Who are you?

NORMA. *(to ELIOT)* Do you have any pills?

MITZI. This is Eliot Iceberg.

NORMA. Eliot Iceberg? I remember you. You're the one who hired that no-good Florida woman. Aren't you in jail yet?

ELIOT. What are they doing here?

MITZI. They're with the tour. Their bus doesn't leave for another five hours.

ELIOT. Do they have to stay here while I bare my soul?

MITZI. I gave them directions to the cherry blossoms.

NORMA. They're closed on Monday. Everybody knows that.

MITZI. They said they didn't want to go. What else can I do?

LEONARD. *(to ELIOT)* You know Roxanne Tropicanna?

MITZI. Leonard, don't raise that subject.

LEONARD. What was she like?

ELIOT. Roxanne? She was heaven. She was just the sort of tall, beautiful, ruthless woman that every small-town boy dreams of. And that's how she made me do it. I made it up. I thought up the whole thing. I designed the plan.

MITZI. You designed the plan to make it snow over the Everglades?

ELIOT. It wasn't even a plan. We were just joking. We were just fooling around. I didn't even want to talk about it. But she made me. She forced me into it. She made me do it. Oh my God, I'm no good.

NORMA. How did she make you do it?

ELIOT. *(beginning to cry)* I never thought she would actually do it. I thought we were just playing. I swear that's what I thought. You have to believe me.

NORMA. Why should we?

ELIOT. Even as a joke, I didn't want to tell her. But she forced me to. She forced me.

MITZI. What do you mean, she forced you. How did she force you?

ELIOT. *(now definitely crying)* Oh my soul is weak when my heart begins to pound.

LEONARD. Yes. Yes, I know that feeling.

NORMA. *(to LEONARD)* No you don't.

MITZI. Eliot.....

ELIOT. I'm no good, I'm no good, I'm no good.

MITZI. Eliot, cut it out.

ELIOT. *(bathed in tears)* I'm no good, I'm no good, I'm no good, I'm no good, I'm no good!

MITZI. Eliot, shut up.

ELIOT. I'M NO GOOD! *(MITZI slaps him across the face. He backs away.)* I'm still no good, but don't hit me again.

LEONARD. *(to MITZI)* What are you doing? Don't you realize what this man has gone through?

NORMA. Whose side are you on Leonard? Don't you realize what kind of woman that was?

LEONARD. I think I do, yuh.

MITZI. Eliot, I don't care whether you're good or not and I don't want to hear any more about it. You understand? No more.

ELIOT. We were together in her apartment.

LEONARD. Yes, yes, we understand.

NORMA. No. We don't understand.

ELIOT. And we were on the floor, you know?

MITZI. Eliot, this is none of our business.

ELIOT. No, no, I have to tell you.

LEONARD. Yuh, let him tell us.

ELIOT. So we were on the floor. And we started to discuss her shins.

LEONARD. Her chins?

ELIOT. No, shins. Shins.

LEONARD. The lower leg.

ELIOT. Yes, exactly. The front part of the lower leg. The lower part of the front leg. The leg part.

LEONARD. Yes, yes, the shins, the shins.

ELIOT. So we were on the floor, you know?

MITZI. Alright, Eliot. That's it. Not another word.

LEONARD. Let him finish.

MITZI. No.

LEONARD. I want to hear it.

MITZI. This doesn't come with the tour, Leonard.

LEONARD. He has to tell it. He has to tell everything. He has to cleanse his soul. I can just imagine those long white shins....

MITZI. We've heard enough, Eliot. We understand. After sufficient time on the floor together, all she had to do was say, "Tell me how to make it snow over the Everglades." And you told her.

ELIOT. Yes. I did it. I did it to myself. I sewed the seeds of my own destruction.

MITZI. Oh Eliot.....

LEONARD. Imagine those long white shins spread out over the bare wooden floor. Crossing and uncrossing.....

NORMA. Leonard....

ELIOT. It's all my fault. The storm. The investigation. I have only myself to blame. Don't you see? I can't go to Senator Orbit. I'd only be incriminating myself. I can't answer his questions.

LEONARD. All night long, the shins lie on the floor. A night full of shins....

NORMA. Leonard, that's enough.

MITZI. You didn't know she would actually do it. You thought it was all academic.

ELIOT. It doesn't matter what my intentions were. I gave her the idea. I told her everything. Why did I do it? Oh, why did I do it?

LEONARD. Because you are a man. And to be a man is to be weak.

ELIOT. What am I going to do? Roxanne will start another storm and then where will we be? People creating weather. It's no good. It's just no good.

LEONARD. Eliot, there's only one thing you can do.

ELIOT. Give up?

LEONARD. No. You have to find Roxanne.

ELIOT. I do?

MITZI. Leonard....

NORMA. Leonard....

LEONARD. You have to talk her out of it.

ELIOT. Yuh, right. Talk her out of it. Convince her not

to start another storm. But will she listen to me?

LEONARD. Eliot, she has to. Think of that night on the floor.

ELIOT. Yes, yes. Surely there must be something between us. Some spark of tenderness, of loyalty. Of compassion.

MITZI. She's a cheat. She's a conniving philanderer.

ELIOT. I know, but she's such a nice one. She has to listen to reason.

MITZI. This is crazy. You should take the plan and go to Senator Orbit.

ELIOT. No, Leonard's right. I have to find Roxanne.

MITZI. Even if you find her, Eliot, she'll only deceive you. She'll trick you like she's tricked you before.

LEONARD. She's right, Eliot. You can't face that woman alone.

ELIOT. I can't?

LEONARD. No, you can't. There's only one solution. I'll have to go with you.

NORMA. What did you say?

ELIOT. Oh Leonard! Would you do that for me?

LEONARD. It'll be dangerous. But somebody has to do it.

ELIOT. You're a good man, Leonard. *(ELIOT and LEONARD start to leave.)*

NORMA. *(Grabs LEONARD.)* Where do you think you're going?

LEONARD. I have to go with him.

ELIOT. He has to come with me.

NORMA. You're not going with him.

LEONARD. Norma, he can't go alone.

ELIOT. Yuh, Norma. I can't go alone.

NORMA. You're not going to meet that woman.

ELIOT. We can't waste anymore time. *(ELIOT grabs LEONARD. NORMA and ELIOT start a tug-a-war over LEONARD.)* Norma, please!

MITZI. Alright, that's enough. *(They continue to struggle.)* I SAID KNOCK IT OFF! *(NORMA lets go. LEONARD and ELIOT fall down.)* Eliot, it doesn't matter that you told Roxanne how to make it snow. The point is that you didn't do it. She did. And this plan is ten times worse than the Florida storm anyway.

ELIOT. It's no use. I can only think of Roxanne.

MITZI. Forget about Roxanne. Did you hear me? Forget about Roxanne!

(ROXANNE and BAGGAGE enter. BAGGAGE wears overalls and carries a flashlight.)

ELIOT. Roxanne!

MITZI. Oh crap.

ROXANNE. *(to ELIOT)* What are you doing here?

ELIOT. Roxanne.....

BAGGAGE. *(to MITZI)* Double-crossed us, huh girlie? Well we'll fix you.

MITZI. Glad you could make it. The gas meter is downstairs.

BAGGAGE. We got you now, babyface. Roxanne's using twice as much stuff as last time. We're gonna have a storm even you can't ruin.

MITZI. Oh dry up, Baggage. I don't need this.

BAGGAGE. Wait till you see this storm.

ROXANNE. *(to BAGGAGE)* Didn't I tell you to wait in the truck?

ELIOT. *(Indicates NORMA and LEONARD.)* Get these people out of here. I have to talk to Roxanne.

NORMA. Hey, I paid for this. I'm not leaving.

MITZI. This is ridiculous, Eliot. None of this matters.

NORMA. We're not going anywhere, are we Leonard?

LEONARD. Well, I could use a bite to eat.

NORMA. I said we're not going anywhere.

ELIOT. *(to MITZI)* Take them outside.

MITZI. We should forget about her and go see Senator Orbit.

ELIOT. Mitzi please.

MITZI. Oh Eliot....

ELIOT. *(Turns back to ROXANNE.)* Why did you do it? *(no answer)* I thought you loved me.

ROXANNE. Oh Eliot.....

ELIOT. You didn't, did you. All this time, it was you and Melinski.

ROXANNE. So what if it was.

ELIOT. Wasn't there ever something between us? Anything?

ROXANNE. Oh Eliot, you were such a fool.

ELIOT. You said you loved me.

ROXANNE. When?

ELIOT. Earlier.

ROXANNE. How many times?

ELIOT. Several times.

ROXANNE. Did you write down the dates?

ELIOT. No.

MITZI. Eliot, this doesn't matter.

ELIOT. Oh, life is cruel.

ROXANNE. What do you want? It's over between us.

ELIOT. I didn't come back here for your sake. I came here .... for the weather.

ROXANNE. What the hell does that mean?

ELIOT. You can't start up that storm again.

ROXANNE. Who says I want to?

ELIOT. It's written all over your evil, beautiful face. I know about Natural Disasters Incorporated. And I know about you.

ROXANNE. You don't know what you're talking about, you fool.

ELIOT. I'm not that stupid. I gave you the idea for the storm. You're the only one I ever told. You think I don't know what you did?

ROXANNE. Alright. So what if I did. A few lies. A little deception. So what? I didn't hurt anyone.

ELIOT. Roxanne, I'm begging you. Stop the planes. If what we had together meant anything, anything at all, then surely you can do this one thing for me. Don't start another storm. Stop the planes!

ROXANNE. It's too late. The planes took off an hour ago. The snow will be starting any minute now.

ELIOT. Then all is lost. You're a vile, evil woman, Roxanne Tropicanna. You're vile!

ROXANNE. I don't care. I look good in black.

ELIOT. All is lost.

MITZI. Eliot, this is ridiculous. I'm going to get Orbit on the phone and you're going to talk to him. *(She leaves.)*

NORMA. What a piece of white trash. Isn't there something you can do to stop her?

ELIOT. All is lost. The world will come to an end. Nature is destroyed. There's nothing left to live for.

LEONARD. What a sad ending.

ELIOT. Didn't I tell you people to get out of here? Get out of here!

LEONARD. C'mon, Norma. Let's go.

NORMA. I want to stay to see what's going to happen.

LEONARD. He just told you what's going to happen. The world is going to come to an end.

NORMA. So what do we do?

LEONARD. What else can we do? We'll have to wait for the bus downstairs. *(LEONARD and NORMA leave, arguing.)*

BAGGAGE. *(to ROXANNE)* C'mon. Let's get out of here.

ROXANNE. Life isn't always the way you want it to be, Eliot.

ELIOT. Goodbye, you cold, bitter, hauntingly beautiful woman. Goodbye.

BAGGAGE. C'mon, will ya? *(BAGGAGE starts to pull ROXANNE off. They are about to leave when:)*

(MITZI arrives, carrying computer printout.)

MITZI. Hold everything!

BAGGAGE. Oh what is it now?

MITZI. No snow.

BAGGAGE. What?

MITZI. No snow over the Everglades.

ELIOT. Is that the latest report?

MITZI. *(handing it to him)* Yup. No snow.

ELIOT. *(reading it)* How could this be?

BAGGAGE. *(pulling it away from ELIOT)* Let me see that! *(He looks at it.)* I don't know how to read this.

ROXANNE. *(Takes it. Reading.)* Ninety-six degrees. Sunny. Zero percent chance of precipitation.

ELIOT. How could this happen? Did you do the same thing you did last time?

ROXANNE. I don't understand this. It should have been snowing fifteen minutes ago.

MITZI. Eliot, I have Senator Orbit's aide on the phone. The Senator is waiting to talk to you.

ELIOT. Well hang up. I can't talk to him.

MITZI. Eliot, there's no snow. You have nothing to feel guilty about. You can tell him about Natural Disasters. You can get your job back.

ELIOT. I can't talk to him. What if he knows about me and Roxanne?

MITZI. He doesn't care about that, you fool. That's just another Washington sex scandle. He's been in three of them himself. But if you don't do something then Baggage and Roxanne will have the whole Weather Service to themselves. Is that what you want?

ELIOT. I can't. I just can't do it.

MITZI. Oh Eliot....

ROXANNE. *(to MITZI)* How did you do this?

MITZI. What do you want now?

ROXANNE. *(shaking MITZI)* How did you do this?

BAGGAGE. Hey, easy, baby. You don't have to rough her up. I'll rough her up. *(He approaches MITZI.)*

MITZI. Back off.

BAGGAGE. How did you ruin our storm, school girl?

MITZI. I didn't ruin your storm. It wasn't your storm in the first place. The storm was an accident. A fluke. Can't you get that through your mushed-up head? You don't know how to make the weather and neither does Eliot.

ELIOT. What?

BAGGAGE. You mean our whole plan is....

MITZI. Garbage. Like you.

BAGGAGE. You watch your mouth.

MITZI. You watch yours. Eliot, get on that phone.

ELIOT. I can't.

MITZI. Why not?

ROXANNE. *(to MITZI)* You're becoming awfully pushy, you know that.

BAGGAGE. Yuh, you can't tell him what to do.

MITZI. And why not?

ELIOT. Because you're the secretary. You can't tell us what to do.

BAGGAGE. Yeah, right. You're the secretary.

ROXANNE. We don't take lip from any secretary, sugarfoot.

MITZI. *(pause)* I'm the secretary? I thought I was the tour guide. I thought I was the business partner. You all think you can tell me who I am, don't you. Well you can't. I tell you who I am. You don't tell me.

BAGGAGE. Everybody's got a smart answer these days. Well it wasn't so easy for us, babyface. We came from the bottom.

MITZI. You love to believe that, don't you. You love to believe it's somebody else's fault that you're a piece of crud. Well it isn't, Baggage. And the same goes for Miss

Florida here. I don't believe you anymore, you understand? First of all, I don't believe half of this crap about
how terrible your childhood was. I don't believe that you
were born in a sewer. And I don't believe that Baggage
was raised by a family of wolves somewhere outside of
Newark. I don't believe it, okay? And even if I did, that
doesn't mean everything has to be rotten for the rest of
your life. If you want something else, then you have to go
out and get it. I can't stand people who see that something
is wrong and then refuse to do anything about it.

ELIOT. Mitzi...

MITZI. Eliot, I want you to pick up that phone, talk to
Orbit, and get him to throw these two citizens out of
Washington.

ELIOT. I can't.

MITZI. You can't? You can't? What do you mean you
can't? I went through living hell for you. I slammed doors
in FBI agents' faces for you. I carried that book all over
Washington for you. By bus. All so that you could get your
job back. And you won't even pick up the phone for
me?

ELIOT. What if he asks about me and Roxanne?

MITZI. Alright, Eliot, that's it. If you don't talk to Orbit
and get this straightened out, then everybody is going to
know about you and Roxanne. I'm going to take your
whole stupid, boring story about the night and the moon-
light and the bare wooden floor and the white shins. I'm
going to take it right to the newspapers. Orbit won't talk to
me, but the newspapers will.

ELIOT. You would do that?

MITZI. Yes. I would do that. If it's the only way to get

you to move, then I would do it. *(ELIOT picks up the phone.)*

ROXANNE. Eliot, don't do this!

ELIOT. *(into the phone)* This is Iceberg. Could you put the Senator on please. *(MITZI picks up the other phone to listen.)* Hello Senator? Yes, it is a nice day. Looks like that Artic air we were expecting has come in just about on time and the warm front isn't giving us anywhere near as many problems as we thought it would. Of course the sea breezes across the Chesapeake are up to ten knots, but I think that....

MITZI. *(her hand covering the phone)* Eliot get to the point.

ELIOT. No, sir, that's not exactly what I called about.

MITZI. Ask him about your job.

ELIOT. Uhh, I wonder if you've heard that the storm in Florida is over sir?

MITZI. Ask him about your job.

ELIOT. The farmers have stopped shoveling alfalfa into your outer office and you think I deserve to get my job back?

MITZI. Finally.

ELIOT. That's very kind of you sir. Yes, a note from you to the president would be very much appreciated.

MITZI. Ask him if he read the plan I left in his office.

ELIOT. Uhh, I wonder if you happened to glance at the document my secretary left with your key aide?

MITZI. Ask him what to do about Roxanne and Baggage.

ELIOT. Oh you did. Good. Uhh, appropos of that, sir, I wonder if I could ask your advice on an internal administration matter. In view of the fact that Miss Sunshower and Mr. Baggage have apparently plotted to take over our entire weather system and destroy our national way of life, do you think it would be appropriate for me to put a white card in their permanent personnel files?

MITZI. No, Eliot. You want to get rid of them.

ELIOT. You'd rather have them arrested?

ROXANNE. You can't let him do that.

ELIOT. That way you can have your picture taken with them at the police station? Well, if that's what you want, Senator. Listen, we're really sorry about the storm and everything.

MITZI. Forget about the storm, Eliot.

ELIOT. What do you mean, you don't care. You're a United States Senator.

MITZI. Eliot, get off the phone.

ELIOT. Our entire atmospheric stability is threatened, and you don't care? This is no joking matter. We work our tails off up here and you don't even care?

MITZI. Eliot!

ELIOT. What about the clouds? What about the air masses? What about the winds? I suppose you don't care about those either.

MITZI. Eliot hang up!

ELIOT. What kind of an American are you?

MITZI. *(into the phone)* Excuse me, Senator. Your key aide had told me that you had an appointment you were late for. *(ELIOT slams down the phone.)* Thank you, Senator. And good luck on the fairways. Watch out for those sea breezes. Bye bye. *(She hangs up.)*

ELIOT. I don't believe that guy.

MITZI. Eliot, you have your job back. Doesn't that mean anything to you.

ROXANNE. I hope you're satisfied, Miss Honeycakes. Mickey's ski lodge will fail. And he and I will fail with it. I'll probably never see him again. *(a few tears)*

BAGGAGE. Don't sweat the small stuff, Roxie. We played our cards and we lost. That doesn't mean we can't look for a new game. What do you say. You and me. A night on the town. A chance to be seen with Rick Baggage.

ROXANNE. Are you kidding? You couldn't make bus fare to Union City. The only reason I let you be seen with me is because you're so sickening you make me look good. You disgust me, Baggage. Go spit in your socks.

BAGGAGE. Okay, Roxanne. I can take a hint. No point in waiting for the U.S. Marshall to slap the cuffs on me. I don't want any part of you or this town. I'm going back to New Jersey, where they understand what filth is. And they know why they need it. *(no response)* I said I'm going back to Jersey. *(pause)* Well don't anybody say goodbye or anything. *(He starts to leave.)* No appreciation. I don't believe you people. *(He is gone.)*

ELIOT. I can't believe it isn't snowing over the Everglades. It worked the first time.

MITZI. The first time was a fluke. A coincidence.

ELIOT. All of weather is a coincidence? Is this what I've invested my life in? Coincidences?

ROXANNE. Well how do you think I feel? I just lost everything.

ELIOT. How can I live with this? I've been leading my life for nothing. When I was a teenager, they thought I was brilliant. A genius. God's gift to science. And now I know nothing.

MITZI. So what if you know nothing? What's the difference? You've got your job back. We're in control now. We can do what we know is right.

ROXANNE. I've lost everything.

ELIOT. I'm a complete fool. I don't know anything. I can't do anything. What was it all for? All the learning? All the dedication? As a kid, that's all I ever wanted to be was a scientist. I played and dreamed with the forces of nature.

MITZI. We can still have nature. But we can share it with everyone else. We're going to change those stupid symbols on the weathermap so that everybody can read them. I'm getting to work on that right now. *(MITZI sits in ELIOT's chair and begins rearranging things.)*

ROXANNE. What about my dreams? What about that place in the sun? That last chance I had to be more than a swamp tramp? To have a nice house? To have a little status? It's all gone.

ELIOT. I didn't need status. I had science. When I was eight, I was an inventor. I invented a can opener that was powered by a steam engine. We would have kept on using it at home except that we kept running out of coal.

ROXANNE. I was all finished with eating from cans. I was ready to dine with the finest. I was ready to meet all those rich, attractive selfish people. All those people I always hated. I was just starting to finally meet them and see how really disgusting they are. Now I'll never see them again.

MITZI. And from now on, if we don't know whether it's gonna rain or not, we'll just say we don't know.

ELIOT. And then I discovered the weather. It was there all the time, but I hadn't realized how beautiful it was.

ROXANNE. That's right. I'll never see them again. I'll never have to lie about where I came from. I won't have to ask a man to mix me a drink anymore. I can just put my thumb on the bottle and shake it up.

ELIOT. At nine, I decided to devote myself to the study of weather. My parents were delighted. They thought I had finally found something that was harmless. I read about how to make a barometer out of a milk bottle. And I did it. I got a milk bottle and a balloon and a straw and I made a barometer. And it worked! My barometer worked! And I ran to my mother and I said, "Ma! My barometer works!" And my mother looked at my barometer and she cried. My mother cried! She knew that I had poured the milk down the drain so I could use the bottle.

MITZI. There are so many things we could do with this agency. We can set an example of openness and honesty for all the other offices.

ROXANNE. Eliot! That's it! I can go back to Tallahassee. I can go back to the gutter, where I belong. I can be what I'm good at. I can be what I was always meant to be. I can be white trash! Oh Eliot! Thanks to you, I'm scum again! Thank you, thank you, thank you. You've changed my life! *(Hugs ELIOT and then runs off.)*

ELIOT. You know, Mitzi. There's something my father always used to say about life that keeps coming back to me now.

MITZI. What is it that your father used to say about life?

ELIOT. That it stinks. Life stinks.

MITZI. Eliot, for the last time. It doesn't matter that you don't know how to make it snow. You didn't want to make it snow in the first place, so what difference does it make. You have your job back. With all the rights and privileges. You have your job back. And together we can change this place.

ELIOT. I have my job back? Why didn't you tell me that?

MITZI. I did tell you that. You're the director again. You can drool over the radar pictures. You can go up to the roof and watch the anemometer go around.

ELIOT. I can?

MITZI. Yes, Eliot.

ELIOT. I'm the director again.

MITZI. Yes, Eliot.

ELIOT. This is wonderful.

MITZI. Yes, Eliot.

ELIOT. This was your doing, wasn't it.

MITZI. You could say that, yes.

ELIOT. You've been really swell, Mitzi. What can I do to pay you back?

MITZI. Well, you could start by making me your executive assistant.

ELIOT. Sure, anything you want. Effective immediately.

MITZI. Eliot, you're my kind of director. *(Puts her feet up on ELIOT's desk.)*

ELIOT. Let's celebrate. I know. We'll have an office party. Everyone gets the rest of the day off. I'll invite the Mouths. They'll be the guests of honor.

MITZI. That sounds great, Eliot. You handle all

the arrangements.

ELIOT. Right. Uhh ... where do you keep the deviled eggs?

MITZI. In the brown file cabinet. *(ELIOT goes to the file cabinet and opens one of the drawers.)* Eliot?

ELIOT. Uhuh?

MITZI. *(Holds out a manilla folder for ELIOT to take.)* While you're there, could you uhh.....

BLACKOUT

PROPERTY PLOT

ACT I Scene 1:
>   Suitcase — In closet
>   Attache Case — In or under desk

Throughout The Play:
>   Telephone — On desk
>   Pen and Pencil Set — On desk
>   Models of Weather Instruments — On desk
>   Manilla Folders — On desk

PERSONAL PROPS

ACT I Scene 1:
>   Envelope — Roxanne
>   Newspaper Clipping #1 — Baggage

ACT I Scene 2:
>   Computer Printout — Eliot
>   Newspaper Clipping #2 — Mitzi
>   Small Package — Mitzi

ACT II Scene 1:

    Computer Printout — Mitzi
    Camera — Leonard
    Handbag with Bottles of Pills — Norma
    Boxes of T-Shirts — Mitzi
    Roll of Dollar Bills — Mitzi
    Tour Guide Hat — Mitzi
    Business Card — Leonard

ACT II Scene 2:

    Cowboy Hat — Roxanne
    The Plan (a battered looseleaf binder) — Roxanne

ACT II Scene 3:

    Computer Printout — Mitzi
    Leonard's Brief — Norma
    Flashlight — Baggage

COSTUME PLOT

Eliot — Conservative business suit
Mitzi — Skirt and blouse
Roxanne — Black suit with slit skirt
Baggage — Rumpled sports jacket and pants, except in
    Act II Scene 3 where he wears overalls
Leonard — Hawaiian shirt, white pants, white shoes
Norma — Lavender pants, white blouse, high heels
Except for Baggage, the characters wear the same costumes throughout the play.